For Daniel and Elizabeth
                        —S.M.

For Shane, Lisa and Eamon
                        —M.O'K.Y.

WE BOTH READ™

Parent's Introduction

We Both Read is the first series of books designed to invite parents and children to share the reading of a story by taking turns reading aloud. This "shared reading" innovation, which was developed in conjunction with early reading specialists, invites parents to read the more sophisticated text on the left-hand pages, while children are encouraged to read the right-hand pages, which have been written at one of three early reading levels.

Reading aloud is one of the most important activities parents can share with their child to assist their reading development. However, *We Both Read* goes beyond reading *to* a child and allows parents to share reading *with* a child. *We Both Read* is so powerful and effective because it combines two key elements in learning: "showing" (the parent reads) and "doing" (the child reads). The result is not only faster reading development for the child, but a much more enjoyable and enriching experience for both!

Most of the words used in the child's text should be familiar to them. Others can easily be sounded out. An occasional difficult word will be first introduced in the parent's text, distinguished with **bold lettering**. Pointing out these words, as you read them, will help familiarize them to your child. You may also find it helpful to read the entire book aloud yourself the first time, then invite your child to participate on the second reading. Also note that the parent's text is preceded by a "talking parent" icon: ⊘ ; and the child's text is preceded by a "talking child" icon: ⊘ .

We Both Read books is a fun, easy way to encourage and help your child to read — and a wonderful way to start your child off on a lifetime of reading enjoyment!

We Both Read: The First Christmas

We Both Read™ is a trademark of Treasure Bay, Inc.

Published by Treasure Bay, Inc.
50 Horgan Ave., Suite 12
Redwood City, CA 94061 USA

PRINTED IN SINGAPORE

Library of Congress Catalog Card Number: 98-60702

Hardcover ISBN 1-891327-04-6
Softcover ISBN 1-891327-08-9

FIRST EDITION

We Both Read™ Books
Patent Pending

WE BOTH READ ™

The
First Christmas

Adapted by Sindy McKay

Illustrated by Mary O'Keefe Young

TREASURE BAY

Long ago, in a city of Galilee called Nazareth, there lived a young woman named Mary.

Mary was loved by many and greatly admired for her strong devotion to God.

One man especially fond of Mary was a carpenter named **Joseph.**

Joseph loved Mary.

He wanted her to be his wife.

Joseph wanted to marry her.

Mary said, "Yes."

But before they were married, a great miracle
happened to Mary. God sent the **angel** Gabriel to speak
to her. And the **angel** said, "Hail, favored one! The Lord
is with you: blessed are you among women."

When she saw the **angel** and heard his words, Mary
was **afraid**.

The **angel** told Mary not to be **afraid**.

The angel told her God loved her.

He told her she was going to have a baby.

Gabriel said, "Fear not, for you are blessed. You will bring forth a son, and will call his name Jesus.

He will be great, and will be called the Son of the Most High: And he will reign forever; and of his kingdom there will be no end."

Mary was not afraid.

She loved God.

She would do what He wanted.

At the same time, an angel appeared to Joseph in a dream and told him, "Mary will bring forth a son, and you will call him **Jesus** for he will save his people from their sins, as has been prophesied and **promised.**"

He told Joseph to care for Mary.

He told Joseph to care for baby **Jesus**.

Joseph **promised** that he would.

Now it happened that many months later, a decree went out from the Emperor Caesar Augustus, that every person should be taxed in the **city** where he was **born**.

And so it was that Joseph was forced to **travel** from Nazareth to the city of David, called Bethlehem.

Joseph took Mary with him.

She was going to have the baby very soon.

They **traveled** to the **city** where Joseph
was **born**.

When Mary and Joseph arrived in Bethlehem, they found the city filled with people. They were very tired and Mary needed to rest, so they began to search for an inn at which to stay.

They went to one inn. But it was full.

They went to another. But it was full, too.

They tried many inns. But there was no room.

It was getting dark and it was time for the baby to be born. Joseph searched desperately but could find no place to stay.

At last an innkeeper offered them his **stable** to use for shelter.

Joseph and Mary went to the **stable**.

Inside were many animals.

But Joseph and Mary did not mind.

It was time for the baby to be born.

That night, in a stable surrounded by animals, Mary brought forth her first-born son. She **wrapped** him in swaddling clothes and laid him in a manger. And they called him Jesus, just as the angel Gabriel told them to.

Jesus lay in the hay.

He was **wrapped** in strips of cloth.

He was safe and warm.

In this same country there were **shepherds** abiding
in the field, keeping watch over their flock by night.
And the angel of the Lord came to them, and the
glory of the Lord shone round about them.

The **shepherds** were afraid.

But the angel said, "Do not be afraid.

I bring you news of great joy."

"For unto you is born this day in the city of David
a Savior, which is Christ the Lord.
    And this will be a sign unto you: you will find the
babe wrapped in swaddling clothes, lying in a manger."

There were many angels in the sky.

They sang, "Glory to God.

Peace on earth.

Good will to men."

And when the angels had gone away from them back into heaven, the **shepherds** left their fields and traveled quickly to Bethlehem to find the babe.

The **shepherds** went to the stable.

They found the baby Jesus,

the Son of God.

At that same time, in the East, three Wise Men saw a brilliant star in the sky. This was a sign that a great king had been born. They knew the star was meant to be **followed**.

The Wise Men **followed** the star.

They followed it to find Jesus.

They followed it to bring him gifts.

Soon **Herod**, king of all Judea, heard news of the three Wise Men seeking "he that is born King of the Jews." And this troubled him deeply. For it had been prophesied that a child born in Bethlehem would someday rise up and rule the people of Israel.

 **Herod** was afraid.

He was the king.

He did not want Jesus to become the king.

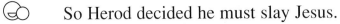 So Herod decided he must slay Jesus.

He did not tell the Wise Men of his plan, but instead sent them to Bethlehem, saying, "Go and search for the child; and when you have found him, come back and bring me word so that I may come and worship him also."

The Wise Men left Herod.

They went to find the King of the Jews.

They followed the bright star in the sky.

The brilliant star in the east went before them until
it shone brightly over the place where the child was.
Upon seeing this, the Wise Men rejoiced with
exceeding great joy.

The Wise Men went into the house.

They saw Mary.

They saw the child called Jesus.

When the Wise Men saw the young child,
they fell down, and worshipped him. They
opened their treasures and presented to Jesus
gifts of gold, and frankincense, and myrrh.

 Then it was time for the Wise Men to leave.

But the Wise Men had a dream.

They would not to go back to Herod.

They would go home a new way.

Jesus would be safe.

And so it was so long ago that Jesus was born. And the promise of the angel Gabriel came true:

"He will be great, and will be called the Son of the Highest. He will reign forever; and of his kingdom there will be no end."

And the angels sang:

"Glory to God.

Peace on earth.

Good will to men."

If you liked
The First Christmas, **here are three more**
We Both Read™ **Books you are sure to enjoy!**

In this humorous and charming tale, a princess loses her golden ball and then makes promises to the frog who gets it back for her. But the princess does not want to keep her promises! To her surprise the frog appears at the castle door looking for the princess and all that she promised!

This lively retelling of the classic story is filled with humor and excitement. Much to his mother's dismay, Jack trades their only cow for five beans. But from these beans grows a magic beanstalk, which Jack climbs up to confront a fearsome giant. Jack must outwit and outrun the giant to reclaim his family's golden treasures!

Featuring the original illustrations of Beatrix Potter, this authorized adaptation retells the adventures of two little rabbits in Mr. McGregor's garden. In the first tale, Peter Rabbit disobeys his mother and goes into the garden, where he is almost caught by Mr. McGregor. In the second tale, he goes back with his cousin Benjamin. This time, Mr. McGregor may catch them both!